SUCCESS BEGINS WITH YOU

SUCCESS BEGINS WITH YOU

NAVEENPRASANTH

Copyright © Naveenprasanth
All Rights Reserved.

ISBN 979-888591061-3

This book has been published with all efforts taken to make the material error-free after the consent of the author. However, the author and the publisher do not assume and hereby disclaim any liability to any party for any loss, damage, or disruption caused by errors or omissions, whether such errors or omissions result from negligence, accident, or any other cause.

While every effort has been made to avoid any mistake or omission, this publication is being sold on the condition and understanding that neither the author nor the publishers or printers would be liable in any manner to any person by reason of any mistake or omission in this publication or for any action taken or omitted to be taken or advice rendered or accepted on the basis of this work. For any defect in printing or binding the publishers will be liable only to replace the defective copy by another copy of this work then available.

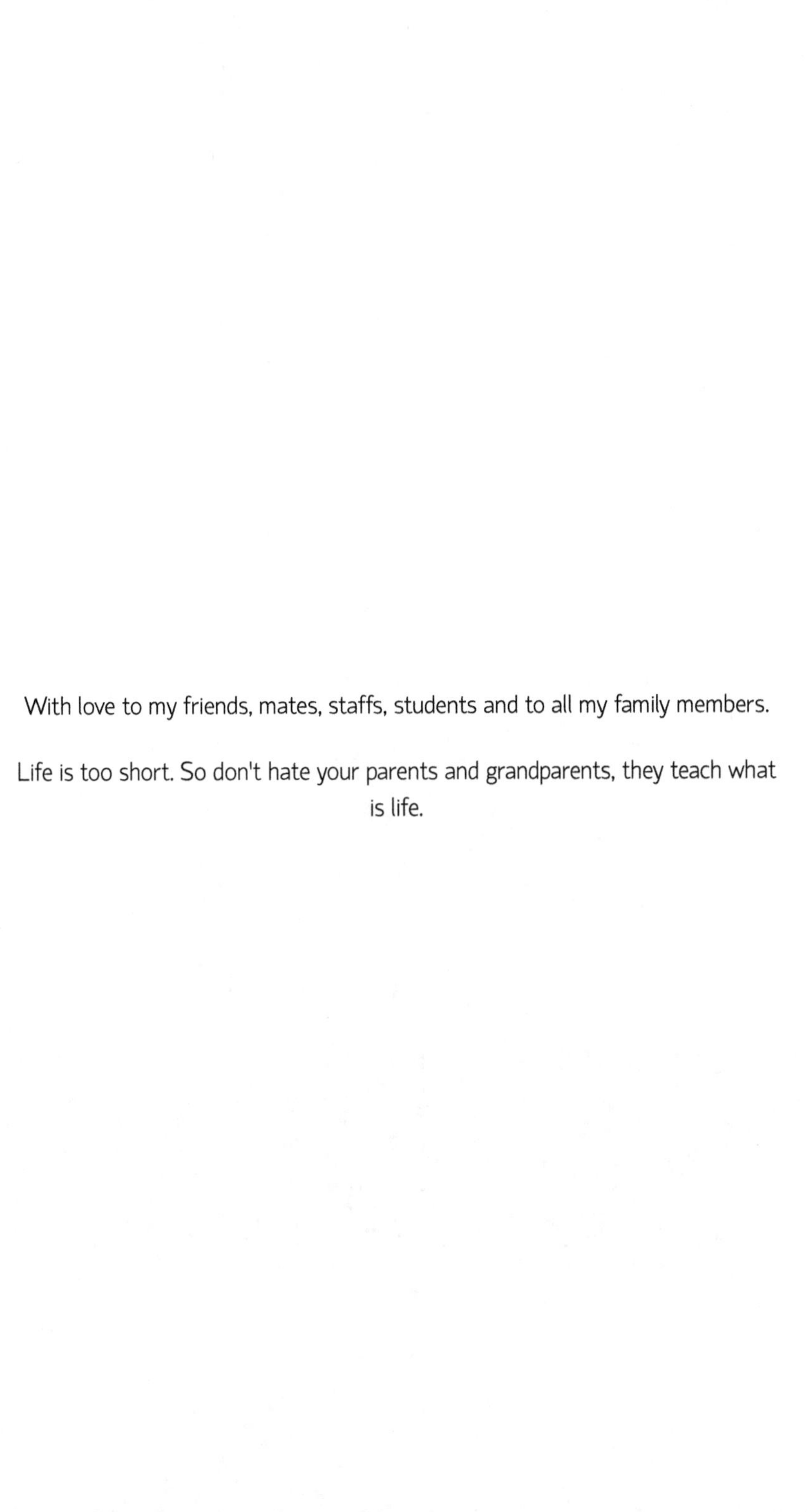

With love to my friends, mates, staffs, students and to all my family members.

Life is too short. So don't hate your parents and grandparents, they teach what is life.

Contents

Preface

Hello everyone!!.. "Nothing is impossible. The word 'I'm possible ". Yeah, this is what exactly following in my life. I have self confidence. I won't believe others in every time. Somtimes situation makes difficult. By following this I received Swami Viveekananda Youth Achievement Award on 2018, Mar 20. Why do i write this book ? Because, every people just having an expectation. Will that expectation always be available. No, What they expect is not always available. So everyone should do anything by their own effort without expectation. Everyone should remember that. Only my own work will left me up. You should remember that only make others think he is like this. Others should consider to be just as good. You have to think about yourself first without thinking about others. Be happy with yourself.

Acknowledgements

I would like to express my deep gratitude to my Faculty members for their guidance enthusistic encouragement and useful critiques of this project. I would also like to thank my co-authors, assistance in keeping my progress on schedule. My grateful thanks are also extended to Ms.Dhivyaa to complete this project as successful one.

Finally i wish to thank my parents for their support and encouragement throughout my study.

Prologue

Hi every one I am Sasika why i choose this, because myself also imperfect before covid. But after this situation i will grooming myself to perfect one. Then i will realised that, nobody is perfect. The one that ever was crucified.

My name is G.M.HARINI I am student at KONGU ARTS & SCIENCE COLLEGE , studying MA ENGLISH LITERATURE 2ⁿᵈ year .My favourite subject is ENGLISH . That's why I had taken BA ENGLISH & now continuing MA ENGLISH LITERATURE.

I had choosen the topic "DON'T TRUST OTHERS". Because ,it relates to me in my life.As I was betrayed by my friend & facing the family problems ,I relate this topic to my life and wrote this story .As a moral of this story ,I wrote my own experience and understanding of life.

I'm Indhu.V. It gives me an immense pleasure to be a part of this book.

I have put all my effort on this work "fail to enjoy the success".

This prose written is written on my own personal experience. "Fail to enjoy your success"will definitely bring up a positive motivation in the minds. Failure teaches people how to succeed in life. Life is full of moments in which we have to push ourselves towards success through failures. This part will definitely build up the positive thoughts when you fail in life.

Hi everyone I'm Ramya. Here, There were many competitor's.. And many supporters for others.. And i had no one to encourage me.. But that time i used to believe my self to sing.. And finally i do it.. In a success way.

My name is Keerthi Thangamuthu, Firstly I'm thankful for writing this content to everyone. I love to read many books and I wanna improve my reading skills. I'm personally interested in becoming a poem writer, however, there are many different opportunities. I beleive that a job should be like a hobby. I have inspired by Mother Teresa's wording "If you really love one another, you will not be able to avoid making sacrifices" and so I like to write essay on the topic "sacrifice yourself ".

I'm G.Amirtha Sri. My passion is to become an artist. Loved to do mandala art. Interested in sharing some positive things so I've used this as a platform and this is first time I've written an essay. In this I've just shared some things about life and the characters which we have to develop within ourselves. These are the things which I've learnt and still learning in my life. Hope you all learn this and apply in your life. Wish you all have a peacefull and successfull future.

I am Keerthi, First I am grateful for having a chance to share this content to everyone, as a student my thoughts always revolve around the idea of being successful and I think it is important for students to be in the path of success. In my case I have been the rank holder in my school and still a mentionable student with a remarkable acadamic performance. "However difficult life may seem, there is always something you can do and succeed at",as said by Stephen Hawking I wish this will become a motivation for all students to be successful in their life.

Greetings everyone! I'm supriya. It gives me an immense pleasure to be the part of this book.And I've chosen the topic "Positive Thinking" which is essential in today's world. Nowadays, people seem to be so disappointment when they tend te face failure in their life.We have to train our mind to accept the failure as we accept our success. When we have positive attitude and positive thinking, we can overcome from the struggles in our life.This part of the book willl discuss about the importance of having positive attitude and positive thoughts in life which will help to change our life in a positive way.

Im Manoj currently I am pursuing my Master degree in English literature at Kongu Arts and Science College. I love writing and reading and as a English graduate I like to writing quotes and aslo like to teaching what I known. Love to write stories and I make short films too...

My name is Aarthi Nallsivam pursuing MA English Literature.Still now I won't have any achievements in my life but My ambition is to become a good professor.The reason why I have choose this topic " Always Failure teach a Lesson" is very intersting and informative because every Story starts with an amazing term Failure there is no other go to Success in a good way only the failure is the first preference of my life not only for every great leaders faced many obstacles then after only they succeed that's what they are in good position.Likethat only the topics inspired me lot to write a Motivated content.while reading my piece of work definitely it could get a clear vision to all Thank you.

I am SARANYA.S from II BA English literature.I am an versatile and more dedicated person in my life...Generally I'm an Hardworker , Enthusiastic and an unique person..My strengths are being positive and self motivated with good communicative skills...My positives are I won't give up my goal for any reason ...From Childhood I would like to read more English books like Stories , Novels that inspired me to take English literature ...I would like to read more and more novels ... And that's one of the main reason I like English literature more...Then after I learnt many things especially History of the English poets ....

I am V Gukashree. It's my great pleasure to introduce myself to you all. I am pursuing BA in English Literature atKongu Arts and Science College. It's my first essay. I like to write stories so Iwrite this content. I am so happy to share with you all. This essay is very useful and gives a lot of information to you all.I tried my best experiences, thoughts, opinions in my writing. Thisessay would help you to discern "Make a good footpath" in life. I thinkthis is the best piece of my writing. This article gives some information about how to choose a good path in life. If it is easy and hard how to overcome it.This essay willencourage you to take a good path.

I'm Denna Christina D . It gives me immense content to introduce myself to you all . I'm pursuing BA English Literature in Kongu arts and science college . It's indeed my previledge to write up an article . It gives a zenith pleasure . I contemplate that it is my strength to create an connect amid the content and the reader . This connect helps them to relate and customize themselves. One of my positive is the ability to stick to the topic and not to deviate from the topic and the theme . This article gives an definite interpretation on the merits of Reading. I have also lit up the motivation for the readers to embed themselves in reading . I'm pretty sure after reading it this would leave you in awe . Reading is a crucial pace in the development process of one 's career. Thus , I have tried to put up the best perceptions , opinions and thoughts of famous and successful people in my writing . This would help you to perceive the title " Reading always pays ".

My name is Pavithra and I am from bhavani I completed my schoolings in Sri sakthi supreme ideal vickas matric hr.sec.school now I am studying UG in Kongu arts and science College My future goal is to be a professor .In the world full of stress there is a lack of peace inside everyone so i wish everyone to find their inner peace to lead a healthy life and so I choose this topic " BE PEACEFUL "

CHAPTER ONE

IMPERFECTIONS TURNS TO PERFECTION - Sasika

Life is not perfect. It never has been and it never will be. But this can be good news. It means we can stop pursuing the mystical, perfect life. It means we can stop chasing perfect skin, the perfect job, the perfect house, or the perfect spouse. It means we can find freedom to live within our imperfections.

Imperfection is in some sort essential to all that we know in life."
— John Ruskin

In fact, the sooner we realize that perfection is not available to us in this world, the sooner we can begin living better lives because of the imperfections. Consider what the ongoing presence of our imperfection means. It means...

We can finally stop chasing happiness in perfection. Happiness is not something to be attained when everything around is perfect—it can't be. Instead, it means we can find contentment and happiness and joy even in the midst of defect. And when we begin to realize happiness is fully available to us today regardless of our circumstance, the better our chances become of finding it.

We can relate to one another in our weakness. Once we fully understand that all people are imperfect by nature, we can stop pretending that we have it all together. I am imperfect and you are imperfect. So let's stop pretending that we aren't. Instead, let's begin living authentic, vulnerable lives with another. For it is in our weakness that we find our greatest commonality and community.

We can fully admit that we need help. Because of our imperfections, we all have blind spots–tendencies that continually trip us up often without notice. These weaknesses and deficiencies are often seen by others—others who can help us overcome them. But not until we replace our pride with humility and seek the help of others.

We can learn to grow through our imperfection. We make imperfection our servant by learning from it. We all live with past regret. And our past will always define our past, but it does not need to define our present. When we begin to accept and recognize our weaknesses, we put ourselves in position to begin learning from them. We can faithfully work to make things better. This world is imperfect. And as long as it is inhabited by imperfect humans, it will continue to be. This realization ought to spur us on to help make this world better. Not only because the world needs our service, but also because we do.

We can better appreciate the good we see around us. The mountaintops are high because the valleys are low. Without sorrow there is no joy. Imperfection brings beauty to the good. And because we know life is imperfect at best, we can find even greater joy in the little moments of triumph.

Life is not perfect, but it does go on. And when we learn to fully embrace both its beauty and its weakness, we create the opportunity to live victorious in both.

What is perfection?

You may say that being faultless is perfection. Well, I doubt it. Perfection is an illusion. Nobody is perfect in the world. Yes, you can be an expert or you strive to be faultless. But, you just cannot be perfect. The truth is, imperfection is the only perfection. Is it bad to be imperfect? No, it's not bad at all. In fact, it's an opportunity for working on your flaws and improvising at every stage. How can you master the art of imperfection? Let's discuss it here.

Our Ego Affects Our Imperfection

First of all, set aside your ego. Your ego tells you that you are perfect. It's hard to accept the fact that you have any imperfections.

Your mind and heart disseminate these thoughts. When you are at work or in a social circle, you are hesitant about accepting your flaws and try to cover them up. You highlight your strengths but you do not want to face your flaws. The result is, your flaws become prominent and dominating. Gradually, it will affect your life. The more you try to run away, the more it affects you. The best way to deal with your flaws is to accept them. Embrace them and it will not bother you.

How is that possible?

It's possible because when your mind and heart accepts the fact you lack a particular trait, you become friends with it. You do not fear it and hence, it will not bother you. You become insensitive to the fear of rejection or insult. When you achieve this state, your improvisation starts. Don't run after perfection, embrace your imperfection. Somewhere, I read some beautiful lines. It said that wear your weakness as armor and it will never hurt you.

I would like to share my practical experience with you. Being a person who stammers, I always avoided speaking to someone. I even hesitated when speaking to my parents. It seriously made my life disgusting. I was tagged as an unsocial person. This was because I was running from my fear of speech. I thought about other person's reactions. Whenever I spoke, I focused on my speech rather than content. One day, I met my guru. He asked me to stop running. Do you want to run all your life? When you'll be old and sick, you will realize the importance of precious life. Either you can repent later or enjoy right now. He asked to confront some patients in the OPD department of a hospital. I went to the podium and declared publicly that I stammer! Was that effective? Well, it had been two years and recently, I delivered a speech to an audience of 2000 people.

Learning is an everlasting process. There is nothing bad about accepting your flaws and learn the ways to improvise. Well, this is an opportunity for you to progress. You should know that you can convert your imperfection into your capability. You just have to be passionate about it. Enjoy the journey and don't relent about the past, you will learn a lot.

Our Spirit

This applies to physical appearance as well. Most of us, judge a person on physical characteristics. But remember, physical attributes are temporary. The only thing that lasts is our inner spirit. The beauty of our thoughts is more important than the beauty of our eyes. It is possible that a handsome man is not good at heart. So, you must realize that perfection is an illusion. Rather than living in illusion, face the reality and work on your weakness. This will take you towards perfection.

Type equation here.

From an early age, I can remember feeling weird and not quite fitting in. To compensate, I spent a lot of time trying to develop into what I thought the world wanted. I wasn't successful and it wasn't until I learned to embrace my imperfections, that I learned they could be a part of my success. I really have learned that my imperfections make me perfect.

"Perfection is found in
accepting your imperfection"

CHAPTER TWO

EVERY SINGLE STEP IS A MILESTONE -GowshiPriya

"The first step toward success is taken, when you refuse to be a captive of the environment in which First find yourself" Life is truly a journey.The experiences we have as we travel through our days gives our life richness, meaning and purposes. In this journey what we do, what we get is based on our potential .

Aren't we travel along with the journey ? Seems to be a tough question in everyone's mind. Let me clear the purpose of life. Each and every single step is much more sensitive and much more important in one's life. For the beginning of our day, "start off making our bed" a general said. One perfect man's first task is making off his bed. If you making off your bed every morning the first task of your day is completed. It make you feel a sense of pride and gives you more courage to an another task and another. And, by the end of the day you can make many tasks. Making off the bed is a little thing but it also gives the fact that such little things also perfects the life. If you can't do the little things right, you will not make things.

"Start by doing what's necessary; then do what' possible and suddenly you are doing the impossible". Your every step is a specific point which projects the life cycle and is used to measure the progress toward the ultimate goal. Till there's lots pressure to live up to certain life achievements on a strict timeline. Your next movement should break down that obstracle. Make sure that your step is as much powerful as to break the odds. Understanding where these odds come. We have got an answer that which makes you really surprise is our society and our weak reactions to them.

Success is not measured by what you accomplish, but by the opposition you have encountered and the courage with which you have maintained the struggle against overwhelming odds.

Everyone should choose your own path. Instead of asking advices from others choose the right which fits yours. Even the worse become better by making right decision in those critical situations. In reality, there are several steps which is split by your age. Just birth to death cycle not only form of living but also in between those crucial time we want to discover more and more.

Here is a short story the great scientist Thomas Edison who brings the glow into our life."He haven't failed several times. He have just found those several ways doesn't worked " He took too many steps towards finding the bulb. He failed as many times. He felt that those are not failures but these are the steps that get him with the right path towards his discovery.

"Failure is the stepping stone to success"

"Many of us are not so aware of the above mentioned quote. As once they failed in their life they feel that it is not be worked. But those who take care of their process and analyze their every step and learn from it, makes them successful not by simply seeing or worrying about it. "Start where you are. Use what you have. Do what you can

"The journey of a thousand miles begin with a single step"

Every single step counts important in our life to lead our life to achieve dreams. To fire the passion of our achievements, it's important to take every important step which makes us cross each destination we need to reach. A man's life is filled with n number of milestones where he grows from child and reaches his old age.

There is a lot of turning points during his era. Not a building is build without the first brick. So your first step towards the future should make your life worth full. Every progress takes place outside of our comfort zone. If we wish for our lives to get a little simpler than it currently is, then we must make a conscious effort to do what we have to in order to make this desired change happen.

We cannot expect everything to get simpler and then do nothing while waiting for it. Sometimes, we must give life a hand in order to realize whatever goal we have in mind.

Now if only we have simple solutions for these little obstacles, then perhaps we could Significantly save ourselves from a lot of trouble and headaches and in turn, be able having one day ruined. You must hack your life process into a simpler way.

As when we are child, our important duties are under the control of our parents. We don't have enough maturity or do not understand the world to take decisions which will one day swap our lives. But ,the passion in us are disturbed by our parents which will continue from our childhood to adulthood or till the end of our life.

Parents' play a major role who gives us suggestions and lead us to a very rightful choices in our studies and carriers too. There are many number of dice(milestone) games to be played between the age of 15 to 25.

It begins by getting good marks in 10th and that makes to decide the group should be taken in further studies. So here, the pattern is already decided by other people where the marks which will act as mouth of snake as in snake and ladder game.

Moving to the higher studies which decides our path to route our success is more important to be chosen wisely. Society and relatives gives us many and many suggestions by thinking that they are routing us in a good way but by oppressing our ideas through their invalid or passer-by thoughts.

Here, our own intellect has its role to play. This is our life and we need to live it. No one can live others life and carry-over our pain to theirs.

Yes, its indeed to prove our identity to the society or others who doubt us through their pecimistic thoughts. In order to prove our will power, we need to take each and every decision like a milestone which is a turning point in our life. We should have a fire in us to wake up our dreams to reach its destination.

It's not a fact that women especially should know cooking and all other household works. The world has changed and so she can go by her own way without any obstructions and anxiety.

Like pooja Chopra who was once an abandoned girl child as her father refused to accept another girl in the family. Her mother brought up her single handed. She proved her capability through many hardships and made her mother proud by winning Miss India in the same place where she got abandoned.

Consistency in our dream, in our path is important because we should not become tired through some challenges that God gives us to test our will power. We also should have faith in God that one day he will pay us of what we have worked consistently without any resistance.

A good example can be taken from the movie like "Kanaa" where Aishwarya Rajesh as Kousi needs to become a cricket player which was the passion of her from her childhood. And her father too liked and lived with cricket as he likes agriculture.

She opposed everyone even her mother for a small period of time to pursuit her dream. Atlast she tried to give up, but as quoted by Siva karthikeyan as Nelson Dilipkumar ,

"This world won't accept the fact that if a man/woman says that he/she will achieve one day instead it will hear the words uttered by person who won in the world".

"Success is the sum of small efforts, repeated day in and day out" Build your own destiny with careful efforts. Even it is, it should speak your pride and courage forever. Complete your progress not let it be unfinished .Once you completed, the step it will automatically pave the way for next.

So do about your work in completing it. Make your way crystal clear by choosing the right path and make the right step towards your beautiful journey. "Today is milestone. It tells you how far you've come. Keep learning Keep trying, keep accomplishing, and keep venturing on through your journey.

So, we should make sure of taking each step in our life as milestone which gives as consistency, persistent and faith which will one day make feel proud of us and others who helped us to reach our passion or dream.

CHAPTER THREE

DON'T TRUST OTHER'S - Harini

CHAPTER- 1

Aadhya was a brave and active girl .she love reading books .Her family consists of 4 members .Her mother Vaithagi home maker; Father Perumal, bakery owner and her younger brother sanjay, studying 10th std.

Aadhya was studying 12th standard, in arts group .Her aim is to become a business women. But it is always discouraged by her parents for them their son sanjay must become a great businessman. Her parents always support her brother alone .They used to say

" Boy child alone will care us in our old-age not you. Because, you will get married & go to other house ".

These motivated Aadhya to achieve many things in education and became a best business women, to prove her parents that even a girl child can save her parents in their oldages by earning money without their life partners support .

CHAPTER -2

After completing the 12thstd, Aadhya decided to take B.COM & for PG degree she decided to take MBA not in same college but in other college .Her wish of studying in her own choice was not accepted by her family .Aadhya's parents asked her to take B.COM (CA).

Hence, after a long struggle, Aadhya went to Chennai for studying B.Com. There she stayed in hostel .There everyone new for Aadhyai the place, college, friends &hostel .There she got 33 friends called AKSHAYA , HARIPRIYA , SARANAYA who are close than other friends. As Saranaya was born in Chennai and lived there, Aadhyastarted to treat Saranaya more than other friends.

"Don't trust anyone until they can prove to you that they can be trusted"

CHAPTER -3

After completing of one year of college life .Now Aadhya came to know all the places.She became familiar with college and friends .Boys can be a good friend to a girl, but according to Aadhya's point of view having a boyfriend is danger .This was strongly believed by Aadhya. Later, she used to take all her classmates including boys in a friendly manner.

Aadhya achieved many things in the academic and also in other extra curricular activities . As a topper, she was liked by all but the true friends were Akshaya, Haripriya, Saranaya .

"Trusting others too much will results in betrayal"

These had happened in Aadhya's life. As Aadhya trusted Saranaya more than others , Saranaya started to manipulate her rumors were created that Aadhyaloved one of her classmate. It was created by her most trusted friendSaranaya , because of jealous .

CHAPTER -4

Earthquake had started in Aadhya's family members life. They started to scold her and even gone to extreme that to leave the college &join in her own town. After a lot of promise &confirmation ,she started her studies .

According to her, Love means not a love that ends in marriage /lust. There is a love between daughter &father, daughter &mother , brother. &sister and even with friends ect.. Here Aadhya got a great experience in her life.

If 50 members started to say something her parents itself will believe it. But that will not happen to a boy. Because according to them,boychild is more important than a girl child . Typically

INDIAN parents will have these mindset in their life.

" I don't trust words ;I Trust Actions "

CHAPTER-5

After completing her higher studies ,she had taken loan from bank on her name and started her business .At first she fails but with continuous confidence and hardwork , her growth was in a rapid speed and now she became a best business women in INDIA.

She alone was taking care of her parents &most trusted son.Later she leave them &gone to AMERICA .

"Don't trust too much on anyone because ,its has the potential to cause harm to your heart only it's better to put trust in yourself and go on your own way."

MORAL ,

According to INDIAN tradition women must first depend on their parents then their life partner and at last their children . Trusting them &depending them is the tradition,not only in India alone but in many countries .

So my request to all women including me is

"Don't trust others for your life, trust yourself .You are equal to men.Make them trsut you and keep your heads high with royal, bold and brave smile in your face".

CHAPTER FOUR

Fail to enjoy the SUCCESS   -Indhu

Failure is must in life to learn thousands of lessons which no book teach. Success and failure are the two aspects of human life. Sometimes we fail in our efforts. Those who fail in life should try again and again. When we fail once, we have experience of failures. We can learn by our experience. Our experience makes us wiser. This is the foundation of success. We get failed so many times to experience our success for once in life time.

We should not think that a man has to fail in order to get success. We must know the causes of our failure. Only fools thinks that success is easy. Confidence is good. But overconfidence is bad. The man who thinks that he is too wise may also fail. Some people fail because they get too nervous. Such people are defeated from within. So they are bound to fail. We must know how to succeed in life. We must be hardworking, we should be courageous and we must have a strong spirit for victory in life.

"Do not be embarrassed of your failures,
learn form them and start again".

Failure is necessary to attain maturity. In the journey of life, everyone has to struggle by facing ups and downs, obstacles and hardships and bound to be there in one's life but what is important is how we tackle them. "Success and failure are two faces of coins" there are people who may giveup or there are others who are ready to take the failure as a challenge.

Brave persons takes the failure as a challenge and takes steps to climb the ladder of success. It is seldom that a child can walk without tumbling or falling down. But these small failures do not deter the small one's spirit. Slowly and gradually the baby learns to stand on its feet and then walk. It is because of the child's willpower that he is able to stand upright. This gives us a lesson that we must try and try until we succeed.

Human life is a long and continuous battle. In this battle many of us fail but we should not give up the attempt. We should try again and again each time when we fail. And this makes us to get to learn some lessons. This kind of experience helps us in our next attempts. We should not ever giveup after failures. But of we stop making attempts after failures, we shall remain defeated in life. In fact, success comes through failures.

When we fail, we should not be disappointed. For instance, Mahatma Gandhi and other freedom fighters worked hard for India's independence. They tried and tried, finally by facing many failures and difficulties they succeeded. Failure should open our eyes we should accept failures and work with greater force, dedication and determination.

"The secret of life is to fall seven times and to get up eight times".

Which is said by Paul Coelho in which he said that each time you get up it will get easier and easier, and you'll realize each time that those failures are the greatest lessons life have ever given you. In our life it is very much important to have a direction and to know our goal. We should choose our career very carefully.

Instead of doing what others want us to do, we should first of all know what we are interested of and what we are good at. It is important to choose our path and concentrate all our energies in the direction we have chosen.

Failure is the stepping stone for success. Each failure will give a path to attain success. We should do our best in every situation and do not worry about the result. Success will come to you at the right time.

Sometimes people just get lucky. Bus success that comes from luck are usually short-lived. True success comes from endurance and perseverance, embracing failure and taking something positive From every failure. If success were easier then anyone can be successful.

One cannot deny the fact that life is indeed a slow struggle. A man cannot always be successful in life, and none have achieved it so far. That is because failure tends to attack when nobody excepts it in different forms. Even a successful men tends to fail after succeeding immensely in life.

"Failures are the pillars of success"

that does not mean one must keep on failing. When one fails in something, dejection instantly hits in. They are disappointed with themselves and everybody around them.

Success is the result of bad experiences in life.

The path to success is filled with difficulties and hurdles. "Bad experiences in life teaches many valuable lessons to be successful". Some people believe that failure is not essential to achieve success. In this modern era of social media, some people have become highly successful and gained popularity overnight by performing some acts.

Hence people have a believe that bad experiences are essential to achieve great heights in life. The success of an individual comes From his mistakes in life.

"Failure is the best coacher of life
So fail to enjoy the success".

BELIEVE YOURSELF
-Ramya

"Believe yourself is the first secret to success"
Believe yourself means having faith in your own capabilities. It means believing that you CAN do something that it is within your ability. When you believe in yourself , you can overcome self doubt and have the confidence to take action and get things done. You need to believe yourself in your abilities , skills and passions to take the leap into entrepreneurship or any other aspiration .

Believe yourself is the exceptional leadership , because self - confidence lets you manage and inspire others with assurance and direction.

i. When you believe yourself , you're accepting who you really are.
v. You're not afraid to give your opinion and you're going to be proud of this person you're becoming yourself.

v. When you believe yourself you feel like you can handle the world! positive energy and a little confidence gives a major lift

THINGS THAT HAPPEN WHEN YOU START TO BELIEVE

1. **SELF – ACCEPTANCE**

When you believe yourself , you're accepting who you really are. You're not afraid to give your opinion and you're going to be proud of this person you're becoming.

2 . YOU FEEL MORE ENERGIZED

When you believe in yourself you feel like you can handle the world! Positive energy and a little confidence gives a major life.

"TRUST YOURSELF YOU KNOW MORE

THAN YOU THINK YOU DO"

3 . YOU'RE ALWAYS IN A GOOD MOOD

If you're happy with yourself , you feel better about everything , which puts you in a great mood all day long.

4. SUCCESS WILL BE GUARANTEED

If you believe everything is going to be fine, it will. It's called the law of attraction .You attract the things you wish for . If you truly believe that you'll get a promotion .

5. YOU CAN MOTIVATE OTHERS

When you feel good about yourself , you can inspire and motivate others with your story .

People love to hear great success story.

6. POSITIVITY IS YOUR NEW MANTRA

There is no space for negativity in your life

You have goals to reach and deadlines to catch. So when you believe in yourself you'll be surrounded by positive people that bring a good , relaxing vibe .

7. YOU WILL GLOW

Even though true beauty starts on the inside, once you believe in yourself you will see it on the outside as well.

8. RESPECT

People will appreciate you for who you are. When you believe in yourself you exude confidence that will make you respected .

These were all the thing that will happen when you start to believe yourself.

"YOU ARE BRAVER THAN YOU BELIEVE,

STRONGER THAT YOU SEEM, AND

SMARTER THAN YOU THINK."

CHAPTER SIX

Sacrifice Yourself   -Keerthi

" Sometimes we have to sacrifice for something we believe in "
What is meant by self sacrifice ?

Self sacrifice is an act of sacrificing oneself or one's interest for the sake of other self sacrifice harbours around self devotion. For everything in this world that is worthwhile, one should pay the price but for self sacrifice there is no paper currency, no promises to pay but it is the gold of real service.

The spirit of self sacrifice creates trust in the power of love and devotion. It teaches us to be compassionate and understanding. No fine piece of work can be done without self sacrifice. The 'father of the nation' Mahatma Gandhi rightly remarked,

"Gentleness, self-sacrifice and generosity are the exclusive possession of no one race or religion"

Self sacrifice is the noblest trait of a human character. Parents sacrifice their comforts for the happiness of their children. Soldiers sacrifice themselves for their country. Reformers and patriots sacrifice themselves for freedom and trust.

Our society is held together only by means of sacrifice. If each Members of the society where to have his own way, without thinking of the comforts and interests of others, then there would be an endless struggle which would make peace and progress impossible.

" Life is not worth living until you have someone to die for. And life is not worth dying once you have someone to live for "

The seed is sown in the ground. But unless it loses itself, the crop will not grow. From the death seeds There we can see the growth of hundreds of grains . Similarly from one act of sacrifice we can spring peace happiness, trust mankind and so on.

The real object of sacrifice is to teach men to give up the best things they loved on earth for the sake of God and their fellow man. A gentleman sacrifice his own interests for others. A charitable man sacrifices his wealth for the benefits of others. A good man always do good to his neighbours. By helping others we help ourselves.

There are numerous instances in history for self sacrifice. Some incidents are blessed are those who have sacrificed themselves to make the whole world free and happy. Many servants have sacrificed themselves for their masters. Wister sacrificed all he had for truth. The Jesus Christ sacrificed himself for mankind.

The Value of sacrifice :

With respect to the day-to-day type of self sacrifice that we are often called to perform us leaders, most of us didn't have any lectures on this as part of our life. Some are those who says there is no such thing as self sacrifice and that we evolved as a species so that anything we do for the good of the wider world is simply to earn for the future.

Many of us, of course, will go through difficult times within our personal lives and are self-sacrificial in ways that others may never know about; and it is certain type that self sacrifice always helps shape us into the compassionate individual who plays an essential part in changing the world.

Time and Money :

Time and money or interrelated because they both offer us opportunities. If we sacrifice them wisely these opportunities allow us to create greater value than we started with.

A simple example that you may be able to relate :

You sacrifice 3 years (or more)Of your life to go to college. The value of the career you hope to obtain from this education is greater than the value of time you really giving up in exchange for it.

" True success requires sacrifice "

Comfort and Gratification :

We all long for comfort, whatever it be the physical comfort of a cozy blanket or the emotional comfort of a loving hug and gratification gives us comfort. However, sacrificing comfort and gratification will give us something of greater value in the long run- long term success and fulfillment.

A simple example that you may be able to relate :

You sacrifice the comfort of your couch to exercise because you know that taking care of your body will give you greater value and fulfilment than sitting in the couch and watching the show of the moment.

You sacrificed the gratification of eating cookies. You just walked by because you know that the value of meeting your long term fitness goals is greater than the 20 seconds of pleasure you will receive by eating the cookies.

" There is no changes without sacrifice "

Ego and pride :

There will be turning point in your life when you sacrifice ego and pride in exchange for the greater value of Peace of Mind and self respect.

A simple example that you may be able to relate :

You are arguing with someone and your ego or prime wants to throw all off their flaws and wrong doing right in their face. But, you know that you are going to feel horrible about yourself later if you take that road. If you catch yourself and sacrifice your ego or pride, you will receive the greater Peace of Mind and self respect.

" People will hurt you, only if you allow them to, don't settle for less when you know you deserve the best "

Sacrifice is the great law of the universe. One thing is sacrificed for the other and this other sacrifice itself in its own turn for something else and thus nature carries on its work. Sacrifice is the pride which must be paid for all progress.

Life – Amirtha Sri

Everyone's life is their motivation and inspiration. Sharing some things which I have learnt about life.

What is life? Life is a beautiful journey where we meet different kinds of people and learn more things from them. We experience both good and bad things. Good experiences become memories and the bad become lessons. Enjoy the memories and learn good values from those lessons. Be an optimistic person.

It's difficult to be positive all the time. But when you let go of negative thoughts from your mind,it is possible. Tips from getting rid of negative thoughts.Use the letter(D²)D²: D-Dot andD-delete. Imaginethe negative thought as a message, keep a dot and put it to an end , then delete.

To make it even more effective , use (TBA) these letters. The message which you have deleted there will stored in the Trash. **Burn** that and **Blow** the **Ash** in the air. Finally take a deep breathe. You'll find yourself free and fresh. Importance of gratitude is nearly equal to the importance of positivity.

Show your gratitude to everyone and everything in your life. It is the beginning of your happiness. It transforms your negative state into positive vibe. Be thankful for everyday and every people in your life. **Thanks for being with me"** say this to your closed ones.

Once you learn gratitude, it will give you more patience, compassion, kindness and understanding. Gratitude will put you in a state of grace. Grace is two things. Intension and attention. So when you have the intension about what you are , where you put your attention. Put your attention in what you have right now. Gratitude should come from the care, heart and soul.

" Be thankful for what you have been blessed with "

Hard work and patience is another key to lead a peaceful, beautiful and successful life. Everyone in this world is unique and equally talented. But not everyone is being successful in their life. The only difference is their level of patience and hard work. You might lose many things, because of your impatience. The more confidence you have in yourself, the more patience you will have. Patience is measured with the level of faith.

It brings to rich rewards. It helps to acquire positive attitude. Eventhoughyou are well-talented, sometimes you lose the opportunity because of impatience. When anger is high you lose patience. When anger is high it affects you physically, by losing patience it affects you mentally. Reduce your anger and motivate yourself to be patience. When you are in anger ask this question (Does anything is going to change because of being anger with them?) within yourself then you will know anger is a foolishness. Most of the time the answer will be no. Then why are you getting anger and hurting yourself. Think before you act.

"Patience is not the ability to wait ; but the abilityto keep a good attitude while waiting"

Hard work is a powerful tool, which you have to use to change your life. Work hard for what you love. While you are working for your goals you may face many obstacles. Success doesn't comes easily. Don't give up on your dreams.

Sometimes you have to be deaf, when people criticise you and discourage you. Keep going. Your success is in your hand, not in your parents, relatives or friends. Choose your desire wisely. Your hardwork will pays off one day.

" Work in silence; let ur success makes the noise"

Love is the foremost feeling that rules the world. Love is in the form of kindness, care, sharing. Some of them will show their kindness only for the kids or their family members or the old age people. It is not the right thing. So be kind with all no matter what the age is. Show your caring towards the people who needs that. Sharing plays a major role in love. Either it can be your secret, or even food (to the needy people).

When you share something and if that brings happiness to them, there comes your real happiness. Example: during festival times or any function times when you share the things to the people what they need (even it may be a small thing) that brings a big smile on their face and it is the real happiness in life.

"Be the reason for someone's smile"

" Share love and happiness "

Finally I wanna say is **"Do good to others and it will come to you in unexpected ways "**.Expect the unexpected things.And the best things will happen unexpectedly.

CHAPTER EIGHT

Be Successful -Keerthi

Every person in this world wants to attain something in life. It might be that somebody wants to become a dancer, singer, environmentalist, banker, etc. The choices vary according to the individual.

It is easy to dream and imagine being successful in our life but the journey of this victory is really a challenging one. There are many successful people in the world but every one of them has infinite effort and dedication in becoming successful. We all are attracted by people achieving success in different fields.

Many of the successful people are also the role models for many people and students in the society. The act of being successful is not as easy as it is in saying or seeing others. It is only we who can make our way towards becoming successful in our life. The most important question that arises in our minds is how we can be successful in our life. We all are born with some purpose in our life. It is because life without a significant goal is meaningless.

We all understand ourselves and our abilities in a better way than anyone else. The utilization of our own ability in getting our goals accomplished makes us successful in our life. Here are some tips that can help you in becoming successful in your life.

What is Meant by Success?

Success is something that is can be achieved by making the best use of our abilities and the resources that we have. Success isn't very easy as spelled but requires greater patience. It totally depends upon us that how we want to shape of life and carrier. Every person in this world has a different opinion regarding the word success in his/her life. It is the real satisfaction and happiness that one gets after achieving the goal of life.

Success brings happiness to our lives and motivates us to do our best. We all dream of becoming successful in life, but success is only achieved by people who are really concerned about it.

Recognize your passion or goal - Everybody in this world is born with a unique talent. It is most essential for you to recognize your passion. Passion in doing any work gives you inner happiness and satisfaction. If you identify your passion and work accordingly the path of your success becomes clear. For example, if you have a talent for dancing and want to make it your carrier then you need to focus on polishing your dancing skill. This can only make you a successful dancer in your life. In other words, it can be said that it is essential to recognize the goal of your life and work upon it till it makes you shine.

Have the courage to accept failure - There are many challenges in the way of success. The people who are really serious about their passion or dreams make their way by facing challenges. It may happen that you might face failure in life while proceeding towards being successful. You must not lose hope but try to find out your mistakes that had been behind getting failure.

According to our former President Dr. Abdul Kalam, the word FAIL means First Attempt in Learning. Failure is always accompanied by success. It makes you realize and learn from your mistakes. It is necessary that you must never panic about failure and have the courage to accept it. Success is a long process and therefore you need to have patience in you. This will surely make you successful in your life.

Hard work – It is always said that there is no substitute for hard work in getting success. People who are talented from birth also need to work hard in their life to become successful. Hard work helps you sharpening your passion and skill. You really have to become extraordinary for becoming successful in your life.

Stay motivated - In no condition, you must forget about your goal in life. As you have seen a spider even after the destruction of its web it again starts weaving a new one without losing hope. There must be something in your life that might remind you about your goal every time.

This will make you more motivated for doing hard work for achieving your goal. The picture of your goal must be in front of your eyes every time either you are slept or awake. You may write some quotations or draw and paste them on your room wall so that whenever you enter your room you must get energized once again. Motivation is a very essential key factor for becoming successful in our life.

Be disciplined and time-bounded – Discipline and time management is most important for attaining success in life. Living a disciplined life helps you to concentrate towards the goal of your life. After deciding on your goal you need to do proper planning for accomplishing it. You have to make time management for everything you do in your life.

It is because time is most precious and if lost can never be regained. Opportunity only knocks once and you must not let it go in vain. Therefore the right decision at right time can only make the journey of life a successful one.

Success requires sacrifice

We all want to be successful in any work that we do in our life. Success gives great pleasure and contentment to us. The process of being successful is not as easy as it is to say.

It requires great sacrifice and hard work. We need to reduce our comforts and work with greater determination to attain success in our life. The most important thing that we need to inculcate in our lives is time management that helps us in doing our work on time. It is always said in order to gain something in life we have to lose something. The desire for success becomes more interesting when it starts giving challenges to us.

Later when we become successful we feel that the struggle that we have done earlier is now fruitful. Being successful is one of the most beautiful experiences of life.

Money and success both are important for an individual. We all have some goals in our life and after accomplishing them we get a good carrier and earn a good amount of money. It is true that money is necessary for everything in your life but only money can never provide you happiness. In my opinion, every highly earning person is not really a successful one. The real meaning of being successful is getting happiness and satisfaction in life after being able to do that what you love to do in life.

A child getting good marks in the examination is a success, getting your dream job is a success, being able to fulfill your dreams is a success. The act of fulfilling your dreams makes you very happy and is the real meaning of success. There are many people in this world who earn money by wrong means and therefore they are rich enough.

It does not mean that they are successful. Thus there is a great difference between being able to earn a lot of money and being successful. Richness is not the right way of measuring success. Successful people can earn good money along with respect in society.

Conclusion

Success is aspired by everyone in this world but only a few people become capable of tasting real success. Everything is possible in this world and people are making it happen. In the same way, becoming successful is difficult but not impossible. It requires several sacrifices, hard work, dedication, time management. The people who are focused and have a keen desire to make their dream come true can surely become successful in their life.

CHAPTER NINE

POSITIVE THINKING
-Supriya

Motivation is an important factor that changes positive thought into instant action. It is defined as a state of mind when everything seems positive and we have a different kind of enthusiasm to complete our work.

Having positive mind helps in many ways and adds confidence to us. It doesn't mean that having positive thinking helps to succeed in every time. But it helps to overcome from the failure and give a confidence to start a new phase. It gives the confidence to face the failure in life. With the help of positive thinking and motivation, we start with new energy and hope. Motivation works like glucose and gives us energy.

Positive thinking is a belief, a mental attitude that admits into the mind thoughts, words and images that good things will happen and that one's efforts will be crowned with success. Positive thinking is opposite to negative thinking which imposes the mind through thoughts on fearfulness and unsure of success in efforts. Negative thinking gives the unconfident to ourselves and it de-motivates us from our goal settings. If one wants to success in his life, he should have more positive attitude rather than having too much of negative attitude.

Positive thinking is reinforced by thoughts such as optimism, hope, and belief that hard work is never wasted. A positive mind will see good in all thing and it gives happiness to oneself and also health, joy, and a successful outcome of every situation and action and works wonders like magic. When we are in positive mood, we could do even a big challenge in easiest way. Positive mind will give us that much strength.

Positive attitude helps individuals create and transform energy into reality. When we have a positive attitude, we tend to see the world in optimistic way and there is a chanced of understating people and the world. It helps to change the behavior according to the situation. It helps individual to evaluate himself and gives him some extra energy to face the reality. It transforms energy into reality with the mindset to seek a healthy ending regardless of the situation.

Positive thinking helps an individual to have a confidence on them and it gives them hope that they can achieve the things. And positive thinking helps not to be fettered by the problems that cross paths with success. Through determination, perseverance, hard work and self-confidence, we can attain positive thinking.

Positivity plays a significant role, and many people have achieved through positive thinking in both their personal and professional lives. In personal life, the person who has positive attitude can have a smooth relationship with his friends, family, relatives, etc. which adds him a more reputation among others. In professional life, the person who has positive attitude can have a team co-operation, adjustment, flexibility towards his colleague and higher officers which gives him a growth in his own professional life.

Positive thinking evokes more energy, leading to determination and hard work, ultimately translating to success. It would be best to remember that nothing gears up people to make wholehearted efforts to perform some task as positive thinking.

Positive thinking is an optimistic attitude that helps individuals practice good things in any given situation. It helps an individual to take right decision over incorrect decision. Positive thinking people will have patience within themselves. So, they will have an ability of thinking anything in deeper way. There is a less chance to take an incorrect decision. It prevents an individual from taking wrong decision.

Positive thinking holds a significant impact on a person's mental, emotional, and physical health. When we have a positive attitude towards anything, it will give us patience and some relief. It will prevent from the stress, depression. It will give us some relaxation, creativity, better coping skills, clear thinking, incredible problem-solving skill. So, it will give physical and mental health.

Positive thinking does not mean to ignore reality or take light of the unresolved problems. It merely means that we approach the good and the bad situations in life with the expectation that things will fall into place.

Positive thinking helps in physical health as well as mental health. Positive thinking holds multiple physical health benefits like better physical health, better stress management, longer life span, better pain tolerance, more excellent resistance to illness such as the common cold, lower chance of having a heart attack, and lower blood pressure. Positive thinking holds multiple mental health benefits like better mood, less depression, more creativity, clearer thinking, better coping skills, and incredible problem-solving skill.

Studies have stated that people with a positive thinking lead and live a healthy life style since they hold a positive view of the future. Through positive thinking, one could choose to become better than they are now. It could develop oneself. Positive thinking starts with us.

Positive thinking is considered as a technique which changes our attitude and believes that we are going to succeed. It helps us learn from our failures, stay focused, forgive ourselves, and make positive friends and mentors. It plays a significant role in every individual's life.

Positive thinking helps even students to overcome their obstacles and makes them healthy, determinant, and self-independent people. From childhood, they learn to cope up with others. They could learn that how to handle the difficult situation from earlier time. It helps them expect good and favorable results.

So, it is the process of creating that creates and transforms energy into reality. A positive mind waits for happiness, health and a happy ending in any situation.

We could spread our positivity to other people by using the positive words while talking. We should make use of words that evoke strength and success. When we encourage others to have a positive thinking, it helps that person to lead a healthy and satisfied life.

First we should remove negative thoughts from our mind. In order to remove negative thoughts, we should magnify the negative aspects and filter out all of the positive ones. We should train our brain to blame ourselves when we have some bad thoughts.

The process of turning negative thinking into positive thinking is simple. But it takes time. When we are creating a new habit, it takes time and practice. If we want to become more optimistic and engage in more positive thinking, first identify areas of our life that we usually think negatively about, whether it's work. Then, we should evaluate what we're thinking. If we find that our thoughts are mainly negative, try to find a way to put a positive spin on them. Then, we should give ourselves permission to smile or laugh, especially during difficult times. We should seek humor in everyday happenings, when we can laugh at life, we feel less stressed.

We need to change our attitude and believe that we are going to succeed. We need to implement positive thinking techniques that help us learn from our experience. Always stay on guard and replace our negative thoughts with constructive, positive reviews.

CHAPTER TEN

Sharp your knowledge -Manoj

All human beings animals and living things in the world near knowledge it is the first and foremost in for everything to Survival animals for counter attack human beings for living in society all the livings facing problems in their life but they need to rectify they need knowledge.

What is knowledge? Is nothing but how we approach the problem and how we tackle the thing but actually knowledge is everything but we can gain by learn and experience many things everyday give some knowledge but how actually we get it.

"Knowledge gain through experience"

Developing knowledge is actually not everything but it depends upon the people opinion some may eager to get their knowledge to show them as wiser than other people but some people not so that much of interest. Because they lost interest in learning something new but updating knowledge is a common thing but some won't understand it. Sir Francis bacon who published the work of being "knowledge itself power" for being knowledge person they need to know learn from many sources to be wiser.

Knowledge is everywhere in the world but people who are interested in their own life will collect knowledge according to their thirst.

People who will collect and search for knowledge will improve the real life. In this modern world people who are learnt many things don't each other people also. Likewise there are many things present nowadays to learn and there are many things present here to teach how to use knowledge on how to apply to from olden days to till now.

Books contribute a lot to the knowledge because the books are the best companion of knowledge previous day people will make time for study but in this modern day's people don't make that much of time for study are they lost interest for studies.

Knowledge is Power why it is called so? In the universe man is a weaker than animals we cannot see the eagle as for, you cannot lift much weight like some animals, but he is more powerful because of intelligent he can control other animals by using knowledge. His education and complete control of his life by using the strength of power why any knowledge is to get awareness with help us to pass the knowledge through next generation to make them awareness knowledge makes the human to think dynamically and you different angles man is not always powerful be always powerful because she loses intelligent to make him powerful to gain knowledge.

"To improve your life knowledge improve your knowledge"

Age is not important the most important is how we gain for that particular age. Knowledge definitely makes our life upward. Knowledge people can everywhere because they can get knowledge & their approach different things. The value of knowledge sharing make you're wiser every day. Never make selfish with your knowledge because give one knowledge will help others people to improve more and more. Grab all the knowledge that is available in your footsteps on never leave anything behind. To improve our life is now to open ourselves for be to learn something whatever comes in.

Because human life is created for getting on making at their own way everyone is getting wiser day by day because of knowledge sharpness and their usage. People will definitely accept your answer when you are different from their approach.

Knowledge will help the human to overcome their weakness knowledge tell us what is wrong and what is right. Knowledge will give up the confident where to overcome the difficulties. Knowledge is a very important tool to make positive in our society. Knowledge is piller of success.

"Knowledge is a progress of gaining day by day"

Knowledge is nothing but an area of known. From the modern age to Stone Age man continued to struggle for going to unknown. He explored seven seas; depth of water, the high skies, the space beyond our galaxy, the human body is most of the entire human mind. At first the struggle a lot but now they are getting busy to attend knowledge. Knowledge for selfish wins results in birth and evil.

The greatest novel yet to be written on the most profound poem is yet to be composed the best painting yet to be made. There is no perfect example of every road and Highway or a government functioning in most efficient way as possible. In olden days there is having some respect to the knowledge. People because they guide others also this help other people believe their words as truth and make them to follow.

In this world people are born with some level of knowledge. Where they grow of knowledge depends upon their environment on how they ready to learn day by day learning and experience make them knowledge and Wiser.

"Knowledge is appreciated"

For people who is ready adapting themselves day by day for the knowledge and they can't stop that progress because knowledge is a vast area and covers all the area. For learners everyday make use of them for their knowledge updation.

Where knowledge is a powerful weapon when we use against the enemy which destroys them mentally and physically. For the people who is born with nothing if the people will earn anything through the knowledge. Knowledge does not by any rent in shop it is learning things knowledge differ from people to people and their approaches are also vary sharp your knowledge.

Some ways to improve your knowledge:

Attend Seminars: Seminars are the best ways to improve knowledge because the person who is conducting seminars will share their knowledge to the wide area of people because of their experience. It is best way to learn comparing study.

Schedule a time to learn: learning is a part of updating knowledge where a we don't need to study all time. Before that we need to fix particular time for learning to enrich our knowledge. This will help really.

Be willing to change: People will not accept changing because of fear and they will live in the comfortable zone. They never welcome new thing to their world because of fear on new thing will May leads to failure. Mainly they are making fear of not accepting new thing.

Be focused: In this modern world there are many things makes the people to distract easily like cell phones televisions social media and many more. They forget what they are going to do. So to gain knowledge we must focus on the knowledge how to gain. Without focus couldn't achieve anything.

Be Updated: For being a good human updating knowledge is more important thing. Because day to day life there are more and more thing happening in everyday life so only update our knowledge foe being wiser.

Never stop practicing: To gain our knowledge not happened in a day. It may happened only by practicing every day. And never stop to learn and never stop practicing.

Knowledge Management:

Knowledge management is the collection of methods relating to creating sharing using and managing the knowledge and information of an organization. It refers to multidisciplinary approach to achieve organizational objectives by making. Knowledge management efforts typically focus on organizational objectives such as improved performance competitive advantage innovation the sharing of lessons learned integration and continuous improvement of the organization.

"Knowledge is a power to rule"

The purpose of the knowledge management process is to share perspectives ideas experience and information to ensure that these are available in the right time to be enabled informed decisions and to improve efficiency by reading the need to rediscover knowledge.

A knowledge management process is the way in which a business manages knowledge including its capture storage organization verification security distribution and use.

Once a person gets power of knowledge they don't need fear of from other power. Knowledge plays a great role in all aspects of the life by let us know the easy and effective ways to solve the circumstances knowledge is a powerful factor which helps us to easily get name fame success power and position in the life.

We can say that money and physical strength also important tools of power; however both of them are not so powerful like knowledge. Knowledge and learning are to essential prerequisites for prosperity and growth in life.

"To guide others improve your knowledge"

Only few people in the world understand the power of knowledge. Every educated person is not knowledgeable but every knowledgeable person is educated. Where the statement looks wired but it's true. In this world everyone is almost educated but they still do not have knowledge of subject that they have studied.

Besides knowledge is something that helps you to drive a car ride a bike solves a puzzle etc. knowledge is something that prevents us from making same mistake twice. It is not something that you can buy from you have to earn it.

Knowledge is a very important tool to get positive changes in society or country. Knowledge gives us a vision of our future and what we can do in it. All the countries in the world that use technologically developed tools and machinery and many other things is the result of knowledge. Weapons and bomb do not make a country powerful but knowledge does. Educated persons can easily handle things in life. It also helps us to overcome our weakness faults as well as how to face difficulties in life with confidence and control on them as soon as possible.

Knowledge makes the person more powerful by giving him mental and moral advancement in the life. In short knowledge keeps peace in the society by keeping people away from the fight and other social evils.

Knowledge is a human capacity to identify and accept the truth however it can be used for positive well being as well as negative purposes. Thus gives the power to create and destroy the same time.

Knowledge can be used for personal growth as well growth community state and nation. However some people use knowledge negativity leading to the harm of individuals or society on the whole.

"Sharp your knowledge for shine"

CHAPTER ELEVEN

ALWAYS FAILURE TEACH A LESSON -Arthi

"The secret of life is to fall seven times and
to get up with eight times "
-Paulo Coelho

The right path to success is paved with failure and the successful people can fall at many times to climb up high In every people life achieving a success is impossible without the sense of failure. The important lessons in people life are learned from failure. Not only Success teach a lesson even though failure is the previous thing which teach a good lesson of ourselves.

When a person can fall down and himself back that time the person can learn many things like they motivated by themselves and build a great strength among themselves.

Every time failure is a key process of a person to become a better thinker and problem Solver. "

Failure is a key process, You need to learn how to pick yourself back up"

Without knowing the value of failure the person could not learn how to succeed. The hardest and the good lessons are comes from only our failures, when one works to reach their success that times they work hard to achieve it but suddenly when the term failure arises in their achievement the full focus of the person will be turn into only that failure again they won't concentrate on their achieving path of success ,the better thing in human life is need to build is accepting the failure and stepping onto the success.

If everyone can start by looking a failure as a good lesson that times they definitely win in their achievement game.

In other words failure is an part of journey which lead towards success each and every people life they fall at one time or another time but the courage is only they learned from that failure and still continue to try. A real conclusion of life is failure is a expensive talent of a person to learn a good lesson.

"A smart Man makes a mistakes but they learn from it and never makes a same mistakes again."

It is impossible to live without a failure. For example when a person concentrate on their succeeding path to achieve a goal that time they rejected for many times but their hard work and dedication of failure paid off and takes them into a greater to become a wealthiest in the world.

The difference between success and failure is simple because only the person determination is to turn failure into life lessons that strengthen their resolve.

The Best example is from Indian history, The war between Prithvi Raj Chauhan and Muhammad Ghori,chauhan 17 times wins in the battle but every time his generous lead to success but Muhammad Ghori Still didn't lose hope and giving a surprise to the he won against Prithvi Raj at 18th times this reveals that always failure teach a good lesson.

" Winners are not afraid of losing but losers are afraid. Failure is part of the success process, people who avoid failure also avoid success."

Failure can be a great source of Motivation it helps to achieve the person goal which push them to work harder until they achieve their dreams Failure is not final, when a person experiencing a failure they thought that the entire world has come to an end but the real fact is that after facing the failure they learn a beautiful lesson and they need to trust that failure is not final.

Failure is an success key which is to overcome and go on to achieve a greater success.

Failure also teach to stay humble in every perspectives of life.

Failure is a painful experiences that no one need to go through it but the truth of the failure is inevitable ,the pain comes from the failure is an valuable lessons, which takes the person into an positive ways so failure is the key to success.

One who doesn't worried about the failure they will reach a high point in their career as Successful person.

A person doesn't led failure into the heart and don't led success to the head.

**"Every failure brings with the
seed of an equivalent success."**

Failure Spreads creativity ,tenacity and motivation it brings the person to become more stronger.

Every failure contains a certain amount of goodness it boost their sense of determination and build self-esteem.

Failure is life's greatest teacher because in order to grow high the people need a failure it is an life's ultimate lesson. Failure only makes is to rethink, reconsider and find a new ways to achieve our goals.

"Try

Fail

Learn

Repeat."

This is the four major powerful weapon which brings the person in a succeeding path.

The path to success is faced with many hurdles and problems. Bad experiences only teach a valuable lessons. The important celebrated personalities in the world are failed multiple times after that only they learn a lesson and achieve in the life.

*" Every successful attempt depends
upon the backbone of failure"*

Experience makes Perfect
-Saranya

There are many tasks and activities we do. Some are easy and others may be difficult but nothing is impossible. If we need to succeed in a particular field we must have **enough interest** and must possess quality of determination with the high level of try in a particular field.

- After all practice makes you perfect and here experience certainly counts.

- Life is not an easy way.

- Everything in life comes with a cost.

- Everyone is made up of experience.

If one wants to succeed in life that they must put effort to achieve it.

Even when it goes wrong or failed, we should not give up because **every bad experience shapes us in many ways** and brings us to achieve many more in various fields.

It is required to put effort continuously to excel in the field. No one is born as an export expert; everybody got their best designation only by a continuous effort even when it fails because at the end it it's not a matter **the success after constant effort only speaks.**

"Life is a series of experience, each one of which makes us
bigger, even though sometimes it is hard to realize this"

We can take and simple example where the **Goldsmith** only perfectshis skills through lots and lots of practice and by experience only ,he succeeded in his profession.

Major Dhyan Chand one of the greatest hockey player made himself perfect in the sport.He was able to achieve this level of perfection in his field only by his experience and constant practicing.

- The practice makes a man perfect but the one which makes a man expert is experience.

A skillful dancer and a famous singer was never an expert by their birth. It's their attitude of not giving up. Always try to teach this habit and concentrate only on constant efforts and not on the result.

Whatever the results may be, it might be a positive ending or even a bad experience; we must keep on trying our best because **experience makes a man perfect.**

By constantly doing our work and with the experience gained we can easily shine in our own path.

"Learn from every mistake because it every experience
Particularly your mistakes or there to teach you and force you
into being more of who you are"

As said above, we have to learn from every mistakes because the mistakes what we made will teach and make us to find our self whom we are. Every experience in the life is there to teach us something we need to know to get forward.

- We should not regret anything in life. **If it is good, it's fine when it is bad it will be the experience** what we wanted for.

- The journey of life gives many experiences. So enjoy the journey of life and collect the experience and makes you so perfect.

In a simple example,
To become a writer, personal experience is important. It will be more convincing to others if we write something inspired by the personal experience and it will be more unique and interesting.
With the quote:
"Be brave take risk nothing can substitute experience"

Pentagon: "Be brave take risk nothing can substitute experience"

I am concluding that whatever the tasks or work me must constantly put effort whatever the results may be experience alone matters because every experience shapes us in an better way and makes a man perfect.

CHAPTER THIRTEEN

Make a good footpath -Guka Shree

" The world is yours "-Was a great saying and it speaks about great responsibility. It means you have the opportunity, the ability, the freedom, to do anything that you want anything that is set in your mind. To take hold of the world or direction in your life or reach your destination you need to choose a good path.

To choose a good path we need to see more obstacles. For example, A teacher asked her twelfth students what are the courses that you going to choose. All students answered. Now the teacher asked who are all interested to take that course but only a few students raised their hands. The teacher asked why others are not choosing the course that they are interected in. The students replied that there is no scope in the course that we are interested in, and there is a problem in getting the jobs. so wc do not choose the course that we are interested in.

The teacher said that I am going to say a story for you all. Once a time, there is a research by choosing a set of interested students taking their course. And another set of interested students that choose the course based on the scope during that time. And they are not interested in that courses.

The master observes both the batches, grades are good at the starting time. After getting the job, the interested student's growth increases randomly and their creativity also increases. Because they liked the course. But the students who choose their courses based on their scope, their growth remains at the same level. The growth is only below average. Because they have no interest in that job. Their creativity is also less.

And the story tells us when we doing a work in which we are interested, we will gain more knowledge and we use our creativity level. So firstly we need to decide in which course we are interested then only our growth will increase and we will not feel for anything.

Likewise, we need to choose the good paths in our life. We have to choose our own path in life. Some choose the easy one. Some choose

the hard one. Some go for greatness and pursue their dreams. Sadly, others

don't choose at all. And may not even know where they are headed.

"Ifyou don't chooseyour path, lifewill chooseit foryou."

First, choose your destination. What is your destination?

People without goals are running races without lines. They are floating through life, like driftwood going down a river.

Choose your path and be determined to follow it:

i. Have Goals – Those who achieve their dreams are the ones that have clear goals. Write them down. Make them clear. Tell others about them. Set deadlines for reaching them.

v. Make Your Own Choice – Make your path a conscious choice. Life is full of wonderful surprises and luckiness, but don't let life dictate your path. Choose your destination and chart your course. Sometimes you have to blaze a path that hasn't been previously travelled.

v. Pay the Price – Make sure you know what you are willing to pay for your dream. Every path has a price. Whether it is years of practice or a certain school degree. Make sure you are willing to pay for your path in time, effort, and sacrifice.

v. Don't Give Up – No one is successful immediately or on their first try. Those who end up winning are usually those who persist longer than others. They continue long after everyone else has quit. Winners do what others are not willing to do.

Choose Your Way:

- There is nothing worse than not having a path.
- A purpose. A goal.
- Choose your path wisely.
- Be determined.
- And be willing to pay the toll for the path you choose.

For making our life good we need to overcome more obstacles. For example, In ancient times, a king had his men place a boulder on a roadway. He then hid in the bushes and watched to see if anyone would move the boulder out of the way. Some of the king's wealthiest merchants and courtiers passed by and simply walked around it.

Many people blamed the King for not keeping the roads clear, but none of them did anything about getting tha e stone removed.

One day, a peasant came along carrying vegetables. Upon approaching the boulder, the peasant laid down his burden and tried to push the stone out of the way. After much pushing and straining, he finally managed.

After the peasant went back to pick up his vegetables, he noticed a purse lying in the road where the boulder had been. The purse contained many gold coins and note from the King explained that the gold was for the person who removed the boulder from the road.

In this story, we need to understand that every obstacle that we come across allows us to improve our circumstances, and while the lazy complain, others are creating opportunities through their kind hearts, generosity, and willingness to get things done.

We need to choose the right path or wrong path, which varies from person to person. If we choose the hard path how to overcome it. The hard path is the one full of chaos which is where we have to make sacrifices, confront our fears often finding ourselves in a fog of uncertainty. Sure there are variations of an easy path and hard ones but when we boil it down to the fundamental truth, we often know the right path to take but we often struggle with making a decision or a choice because the path we need to take is often a gruelling one fraught with obstacles, unknowns and hard work. Backbreaking work.Gut-wrenching courage. Whether we are trying to repair a fragile relationship with a loved one or move across the country make a major career shift or start a new business, choosing the hard path is not our first choice. The the hard path is often the one that we need to be on but doesn't choose because of the fear of failure.

Hard is where we experience failure, pain, suffering, rejection and the sickness of uncertainty. Hard teaches us about others...who our friends are. Hard teaches us about ourselves and what we are willing to do to live a full life. Hard is how we learn that the best part of ourselves is often hidden deep inside ready to come out and be put to a greater purpose.

"Hardisthe way forward.
Everything worth doing is hard.
Everything worth doing requires effort.
Everythingworthbecomingishard."

Choosing the right path these days can be difficult because they all look hard. But the good news is that...You can handle the hard path.

Choose the right path whether it is hard or easy. If it is hard, overcome it the life makes it as easy one. The right path leaves you with no regrets and no doubts, eventually leading you to a purpose in your life.

Don't compare your path with anybody .your path is unique to you. Life is

what you make it. Find your path to fulfilment.

" Make a good footpath, instead of following one already made."

I am concluding this essay with time stands at the centre of your life. You never feel like you have enough of it. You want to make the right choices for your future but you're worried about wasting it. You want to find the right direction before the time runs out. you are motivated and ambitious. You want to find the right path and make the right decisions when it comes to your future, but there's the possibility that you'll spend months or years pursuing something you that might not be worth your time and effort.

Choose your path and succeed in life, Life is your own creation."

CHAPTER FOURTEEN

READING ALWAYS PAYS
-Denna

Most of us tend to indulge ourselves in different activities during a leisure time . We listen to music , engage ourselves in social media and many more. But , one of the most valuable hobbies is" Reading . "A person who possess reading as his or her hobby refines that it he or she is preserving a treasure.

" Reading is to the mind what

exercise is to the body " (-Richard Steele)

Who created Reading ?

Reading began life as a Saxon settlement. Reading was originally called Reada ingas, which means the people of Reada. Reada was a Saxon leader who settled in the area with his tribe in the 6th century. The early settlement was probably in the area of St Marys Butts.

Origin of Reading Novel :

In the eleventh century a Japanese women known as murasaki shikibu wrote , " the tale of Ginji " , a 54-chapter story of courtly seduction believed to be the world's first novel.

Nearly 2,000 years later, people the world over are still engrossed by novels — even in an era where stories appear on handheld screens and disappear 24 hours later.

" A book is a dream that you hold in your hand ".

- Neil Gaiman

Father of Reading day :

Puthuvayil Narayana Panicker (1 March 1909 – 19 June 1995) is known as the Father of the Library Movement in the Indian state of Kerala. The activities of the Kerala Grandhasala Sangham that he initiated triggered a popular cultural movement in Kerala which produced universal literacy in the state in the 1990s.

Puthuvayil Narayana Panicker is famously known as the Father of the Library Movement in the state of Kerala. He passed away on June 19, 1995. He initiated the trend of popular cultural movement in Kerala. The Reading Day celebration started merely in 1996.

In 2017, Indian Prime Minister Narendra Modi declared June 19, Kerala's Reading Day, as National Reading Day in India.[2] The following month is also observed as National Reading Month in India.

**" I cannot teach anybody anything ' I
can only make them think ".**

-Socrates

Types of Reading :

There are four ways to attain content on reading . They are the following ,

* Skimming
* Scanning
* Intensive
* Extensive

Skimming : This is referred as to as gist reading, means going through the text to grasp the main idea. ...

Scanning: Here, the reader quickly scuttles across sentences to get to a particular piece of information. ...

Extensive reading is an approach to language learning in which long text and a large amount of material are read by the students for general understanding.

Intensive Reading is a reading method wherein learners are supposed to read the short text carefully and deeply so as to gain maximum understanding .

" A child who reads will be an adult who thinks "

Readings pays in zenith :

Reading is the only deed that always pays you in abundance . It profits you more than what you invest. Reading pays you profusely thahjjn what you put in it. It never ends up in loss instead , it always has excess progress in its profit . Reading books or any other stuffs like magazine , journals , articles etc ....pays you high interest reward.

" To read means to borrow , to create out of one's reading is paying off one's debts " .

Reading always gives us ample of benefits . When we read , we find ourselves in the world of fiction and imagination. Reading takes us the world that the author has interpreted . It makes us a insightful person . It transformers you to a resourceful person .

" In the end , we'll all become stories " .

- Margaret Atwood

Reading always benefits both your physical and mental health and those benefits can last a lifetime. They begin in early childhood and continue through the senior years.A growing body of research indicates that reading literally changes your mind.

Increases your ability to empathize :

And speaking of sensing pain, researchTrusted Source has shown that people who read literary fiction , stories that explore the inner lives of characters — show a heightened ability to understand the feelings and beliefs of others.

Researchers call this ability the "theory of mind," a set of skills essential for building, navigating, and maintaining social relationships.

" Books builds empathy ,

Empathy leads to compassion .

Compassion leads to change .

Books can change the world ".

- Alan Gratz

Builds your vocabulary

Reading researchers as far back as the 1960s have discussed what's known as "the Matthew effect Trusted Source," a term that refers to biblical verse Matthew 13:12: "Whoever has will be given more, and they will have an abundance. Whoever does not have, even what they have will be taken from them."

The Matthew effect sums up the idea that the rich get richer and the poor get poorer — a concept that applies as much to vocabulary as it does to money.

Researchers have found Trusted Source that students who read books regularly, beginning at a young age, gradually develop large vocabularies. And vocabulary size can influence many areas of your life, from scores on standardized tests to college admissions and job opportunities.

A 2019 poll conducted by Cengage showed that 69 percent of employers are looking to hire people with "soft" skills, like the ability to communicate effectively. Reading books is the best way to increase your exposure to new words, learned in context.

" By reading so much , my vocabulary automatically improved along with my comprehension ".

- Benjamin Carson

Reading books pays you in different ways. There are distinct ways to read. It is defined as some books are to be chewed and swallowed , some to be digested and some to be tasted in smaller quantity . It states that some books are to be read on whole , some to be read partially and some books to be grasped .

" A book is a gift you can open again and again ".

- Garrison Keillor

When we read , we become a person with anticipation . It moulds us to be sensitive. Reading entangles us to emotions. It helps you to analyse people around you. When you read novels and dramas , the plot and other subjects enables you to understand and analyse the situation and it's solutions . Thus , in reality it frames us to be a better person to handle the worst as well as good circumstances. When you read a science novel , you gain the knowledge of science . We even become a person to read the psychology of the people. In this ways reading pays us to be a knowledgeable person .

" Reading is the gateway skill that makes all other learning possible ".

- Barack Obama

Lets all intent to read everyday, with the fast moving time . Read every single day to enhance your knowledge and gain wisdom. There is nothing certain in this world but the wisdom that you attain reading is always certain and resistible . Reading is ne the waste of time 9 a boring activity to do. Rather it is the best thing to do which pays enormous virtues . Once you start reading it creates a crave among you.

" An hour spent reading is
one stolen from the paradise ".

Thomas Wharton

It is the person who read becomes a writer in his or her own life. He or she interpret his or her life as a beautiful novel with lots of adventures in it. It has lots of emotions in his or her stories . It takes you to your world. Reading pays us with our own world.

Let's Abstain and become a writer of our own paradise. With the merits of reading lets accomplish more and acquire plenty . Never give a the distinct virtues that reading pays you . .

" A Writer only begins a book ,
a reader finishes it ".

Samuel Johnson

Altogether let us end up reading books and obtain much more . Together lets earn and gain further . A person who has got best books to read is considered as a Luckiest . Now it's your turn to be the luckiest. Are you the luckiest ? Adding to the one who has read the best collections is contemplated as the wealthiest . Are you the wealthiest ? Read more and fresh , be a person with a thirst to read .

CHAPTER FIFTEEN

BE PEACEFUL -Pavithra

Peace is the way which we can take for bringing growth and prosperity to our life and society. If we don't have peace in our life, achieving our dreams, wishes, etc. Will be impossible. I think peace is far more than just a truce. If we are to achieve peace. we must every day make a difference.

"Peace behind with a smile."I absolutely agree! It has said that a smile can light up a room, so imagine what a world of peace can do.

Being peaceful in our life is one of the key for happiness in our life. A peaceful is a life that is lived with a balanced harmony inside you, and around you. It means that you feel content with whatever is going in your life or around you and no one can disturb this inner from yours.

A peaceful life is yours when you remove ego and desires completely and visualize yourself as a peaceful being. When you are peaceful, you are able to think clearly and control negative emotions a lot better than you can in a disturbed state of mind. Peace can make our nation healthy, wealthy, and strong.

Without peace, It is impossible to imagine a prosperous and developed nations. Peaceful mind helps us in learning and understanding things faster. Peace keeps us mentally and physically fit. Peace provides strength to society. Peace is important because it brings unity, optimism, and collaboration among society. Peace increases our concentration of mind.

Peace is one of the important human values. It refers to silence or reconcile. It means to live together in harmony. Without it, society can't progress. It is very necessary for the growth of society as well as a nation. Peace is about resolving conflict without violence. Respect for local culture and belief in the power of local capacities, ideas and solutions.

Inner peace calms our mind and allows us to see our path much clearer, helping us focus and keep track of our goals. Peace is that open door which you see all of your life, but you never choose to walk through that way.

Our life is full of such situations where we compromise our peace of mind. We find ourselves helpless.

We always feel there is nothing left to which we can retrieve to our peace of mind but we often forget that peace is not an option. It is already within our soul; we just need to discover it.

Living in the present moment means to live without worrying about your future or forgetting about your past mistakes. Believing that whatever you can do in life, this is the moment, the present. You can change your past self; you can make your future self. You can fulfill your dreams; you can live without any worry.

Only the present moment can give you the peace, you can learn things without any tension, getting back to the past only gives you sorrow and regrets. Peaceful life not means that the people who is not talking more, always silent which not means that they are having a peaceful life. The real peaceful life is we want to feel happy if we don't have any luxurious in life. Peace means a situation which is free from every tension and problem of life.

No one have peace in today's life every one is chasing some things and because of that they don't live a peaceful life between your brain and your mind. Peaceful life means PEACE within no war inside you between your brain and your mind. Real peace of life is when you are fully satisfied with your life,

For example:

A mother feels real peace of her life when she holds her new born child in her hands and laughs with a contented smile. In everybody's life there must be some chaos with peace.

Though I think we can get peaceful life by follows:

- Don't be jealous. Now-a -days we want to compete with others. But according to me we should compete with ourselves.

- Don't see others. Always try to improve yourself.

- Forgive & forget.

- Do that work what gives you pleasure.

- Always think positive.

Find peace in your life.

Finally, to say about peace, it is a major part our life, even we can't take a single decision without peaceful mind since it has impact in every humans life. One of the fact is humans can't live without foods, shelter, water which is known already , same as these, humans can't live without peace.

"Be peaceful and your life will be wonderful."